Create your own adventure, one drawing at a time.

Author/Editor : Nicole Park, Eva Park
Publisher: AZIBOOKS
Email: azibooksbusiness@gmail.com

1. Poko
2. Pirate
3. Basketball backboard
4. Momo
5. Pig
6. Mosquito
7. Nibbly
8. Bat
9. Skateboarding
10. Bobo
11. Raccoon
12. Trident
13. Tippy
14. Converse
15. Axe
16. Pippin
17. hedgehog
18. Racing Flags
19. Tent
20. The Moon Bunny
21. Ninja
22. Football
23. Baseball glove
24. Roman Sword
25. Nexa
26. Crickets
27. Medieval shield
28. Chompy
29. Bow & Arrow
30. French Bulldog
31. Dog
32. Fighter aircraft
33. Weightlifting
34. Pig
35. Pachycephalosaurus
36. Rolo
37. Winky
38. Hen
39. Cytron
40. skiing
41. Triceratops
42. Police car
43. Light aircraft
44. Snappy
45. Jellyfish
46. Bat Ice Cream
47. Baseball equipment
48. Vampire

49. Surfing
50. Raccoon pirate
51. Treasure Box
52. Pyramid
53. Mummy
54. bat Bunny
55. Motorcycle
56. Frog
57. Pirate Cutlass Sword
58. Anglerfish
59. Excavator
60. Seal
61. Crab
62. Tractor
63. Capybara
64. Cockatoo
65. Bee
66. Submarine
67. Baby Fox
68. Whale Shark
69. Voltix
70. Arctic Fox
71. Octopus
72. Gecko
73. Brushtail Possum
74. Space-X
75. Baby Elephant
76. Otter
77. Hot air balloon
78. Butterfly
79. Pterosaur
80. Compact Car
81. Basketball
82. Llama
83. Anchor
84. Frankenstein
85. Miniature Schnauzer
86. Firefighter
87. Red Dragonfly
88. Sloth
89. Pirate Hat
90. Cabbage Worm
91. Desert Scorpion
92. Tombstone
93. Monarch Butterfly
94. Dachshund
95. Fuzzy
96. Cat

97. Ziggy
98. Starfish
99. Wild Boar
100. Sea Turtle
101. Magic Ring
102. Rocket
103. Astronomical Telescope
104. Parasaurolophus
105. Fresh Juice
106. Cat
107. Magical Sword
108. centipede
109. Monkey
110. Godzilla
111. Wobbo
112. Howling
113. Rooster
114. Gold Mask of Tutankhamun
115. Great white shark
116. Castle
117. Mumu
118. Rhino
119. Pippu(Acorn)
120. Medieval Knight
121. Giraffe
122. Frankenstein
123. Water
124. Hippo
125. Fitness Equipment
126. Roman Soldier
127. Anubis
128. Manticore
129. Parrot
130. Death
131. Handheld Game Console
132. Fire engine
133. Hyena
134. Fangor
135. Ambulance
136. Dairy cattle
137. Alcohol Lamp
138. Witch
139. Triceratops
140. Cowboy Hat
141. Wolfric
142. Lion
143. ChemistryExperiments
144. Dilophosaurus

145. Lycor
146. Fly
147. axing a tree
148. Herbivorous Dinosaur
149. Meerkat
150. Skywing
151. Kangaroo
152. Tutu
153. Angry Face
154. Satan
155. Draknor
156. Billy goat
157. Gingerbread Men
158. Turkey
159. Skull Death
160. Bull
161. Petting a dog
162. Armadillo
163. True seal
164. Chompillar
165. Caterpillar
166. Snowman
167. Scribbler
168. Snail
169. Axolotl
170. Peepra
171. Satellite
172. Pyrofang
173. Surfing
174. a chick watching a caterpillar
175. Gloomshade
176. Astronaut
177. Camel
178. Hauntling
179. Fuzzbeast
180. Crocodile
181. Yark
182. Shagglor
183. Chameleon
184. Ostrich
185. Glaregon
186. Tiger
187. Quokka
188. Swampfang
189. Satellite Antenna
190. Puffpaws
191. Island
192. Cobra

193. Duck
194. Shark
195. Tyrannosaur
196. Spectra
197. Tadpole
198. Woodworking
199. Kraken
200. Scorpion
201. Baby Dinosaur
202. Giant panda
203. Welsh Corgi
204. Marshlurker
205. Viking
206. Hedgehog
207. Spider
208. Vampire Bee
209. Dwarf
210. Eagle
211. Hadrosaurus
212. Puffdragon
213. Mimic
214. Boxing Gloves
215. Zebra
216. Samurai Skull
217. Cargo ship
218. Lion
219. Zuzu
220. Witch Cat
221. Fawn
222. Pirate Parrot
223. Hammer & Wrench
224. spotted ray
225. Fluffkin
226. Kickboard
227. Viking Warrior
228. Mammoth
229. Plesiosaurus
230. Cat riding a skateboard
231. Phantasm
232. Compass
233. Stegosaurus
234. Ghost Pumpkin
235. Scaledon
236. Magic potion
237. Turtle
238. Crooked Witch Hat
239. Viking
240. Gorilla

Let's draw a picture

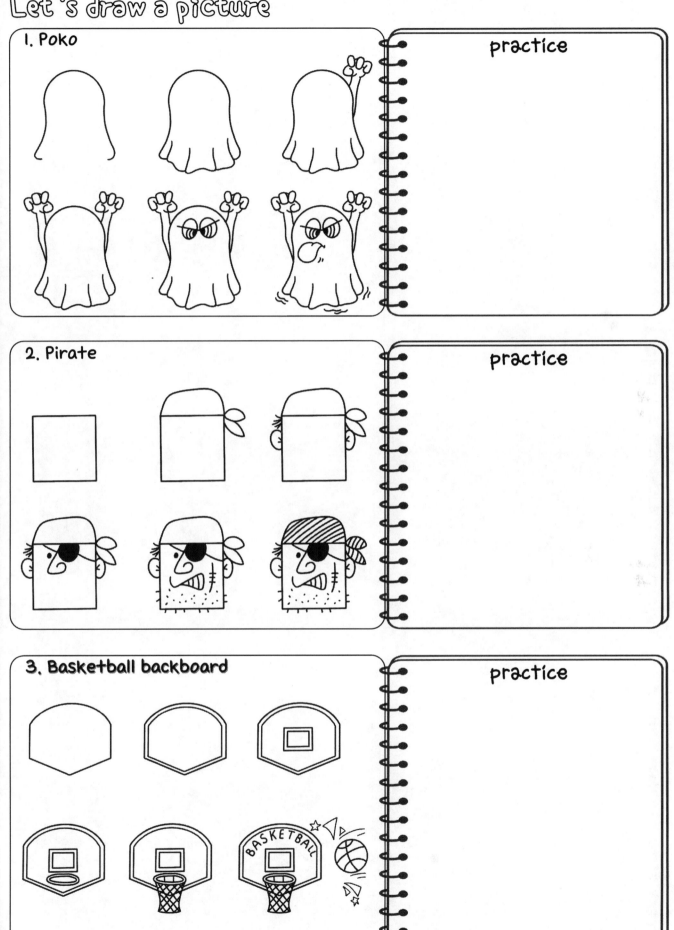

1. Poko

practice

2. Pirate

practice

3. Basketball backboard

practice

BASKETBALL

Let's draw a picture

practice

4. Momo

practice

5. Pig

practice

6. Mosquito

Let's draw a picture

7. Nibbly

practice

8. Bat

practice

9. Skateboarding

practice

Let's draw a picture

practice

10. Bobo

practice

11. Raccoon

practice

12. Trident

Let's draw a picture

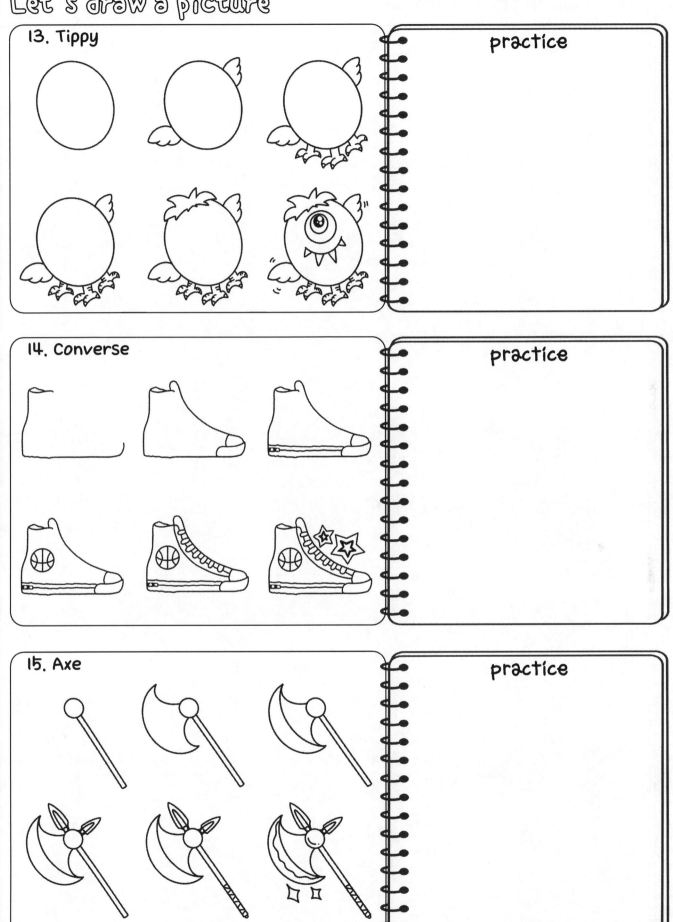

13. Tippy

practice

14. Converse

practice

15. Axe

practice

Let's draw a picture

practice

16. Pippin

practice

17. hedgehog

practice

18. Racing Flags

Let's draw a picture

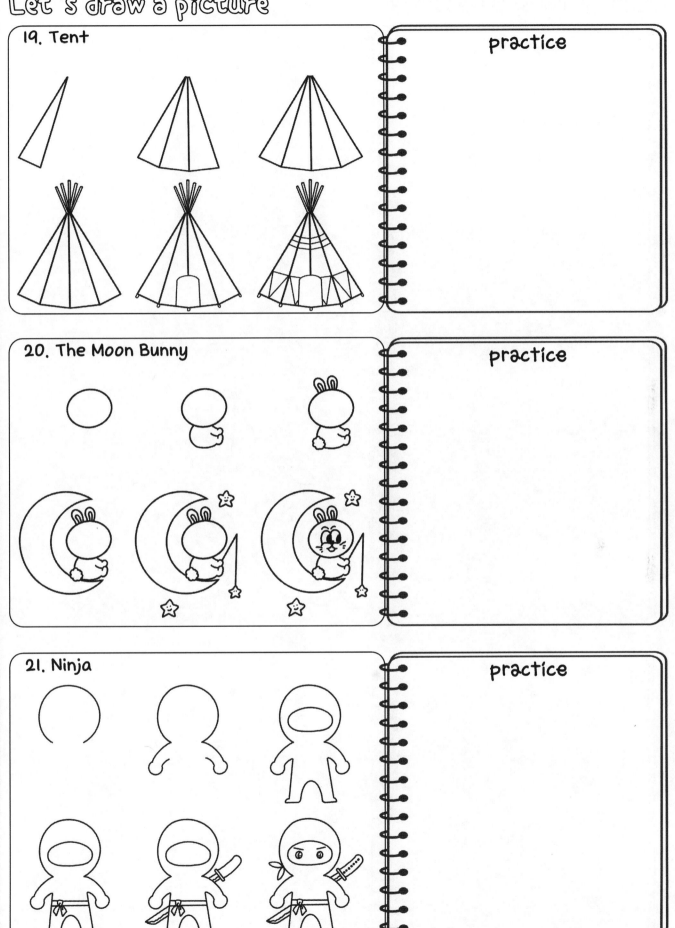

19. Tent

practice

20. The Moon Bunny

practice

21. Ninja

practice

Let's draw a picture

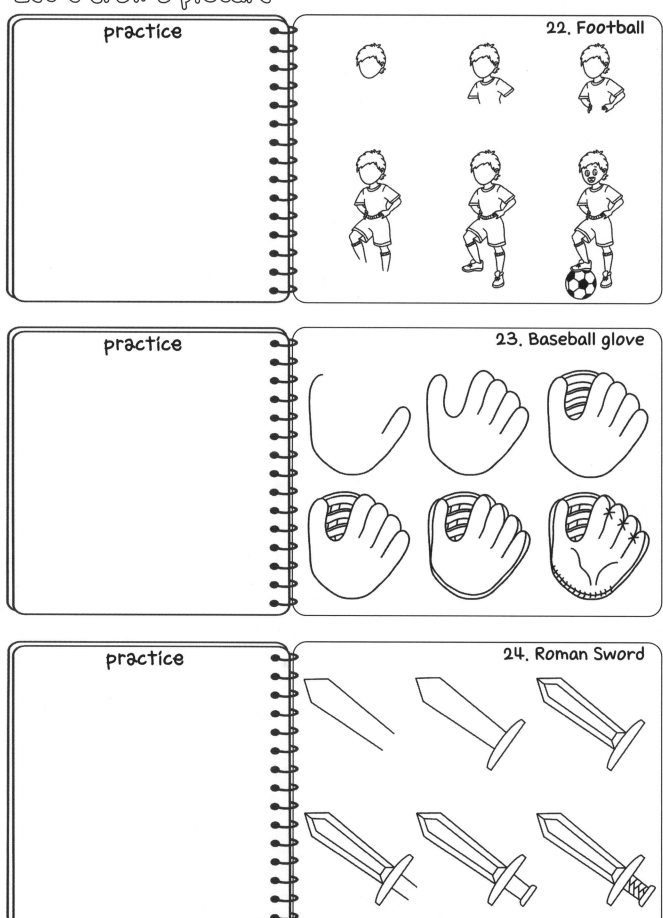

practice

22. Football

practice

23. Baseball glove

practice

24. Roman Sword

Let's draw a picture

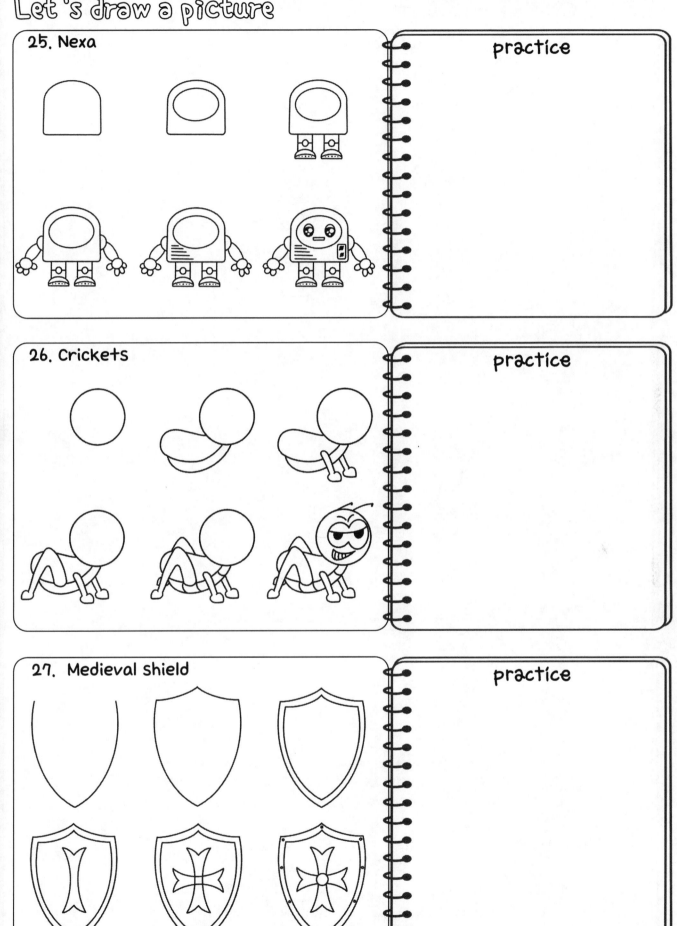

25. Nexa

practice

26. Crickets

practice

27. Medieval shield

practice

Let's draw a picture

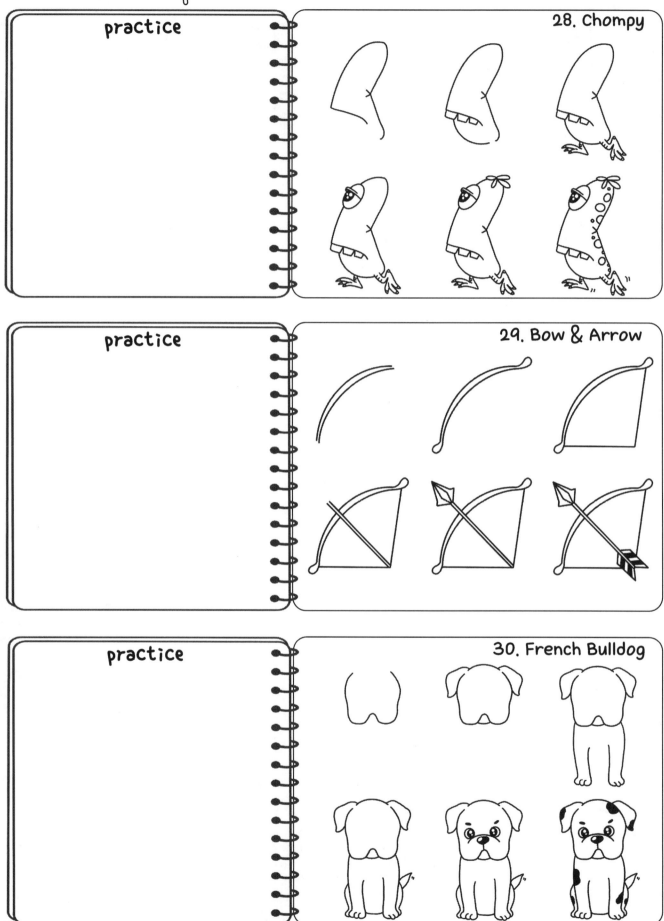

practice

28. Chompy

practice

29. Bow & Arrow

practice

30. French Bulldog

Let's draw a picture

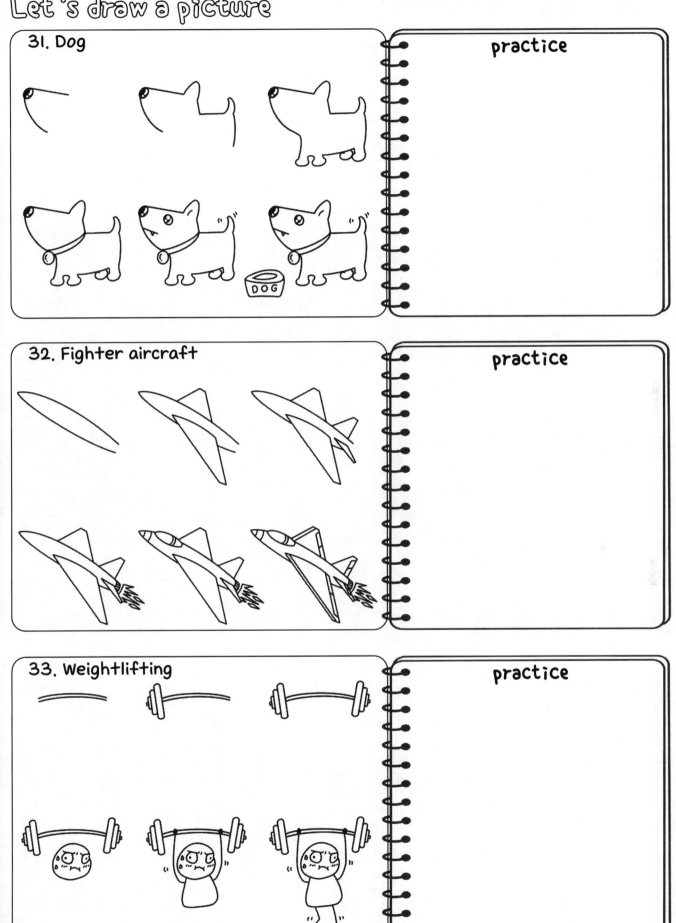

31. Dog

32. Fighter aircraft

33. Weightlifting

DOG

Let's draw a picture.

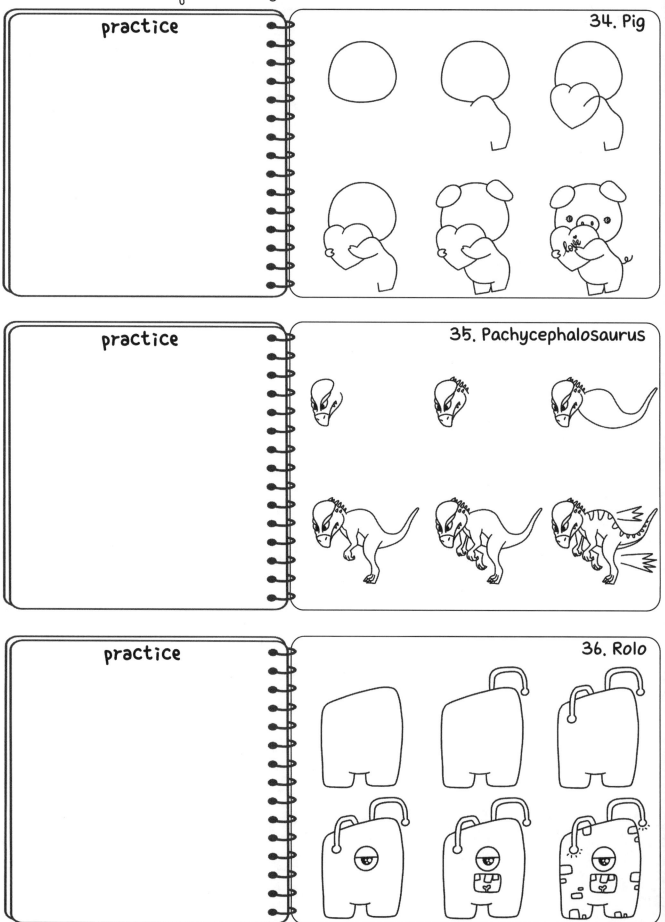

practice

34. Pig

practice

35. Pachycephalosaurus

practice

36. Rolo

Let's draw a picture

37. Winky

38. Hen

39. Cytron

Let's draw a picture.

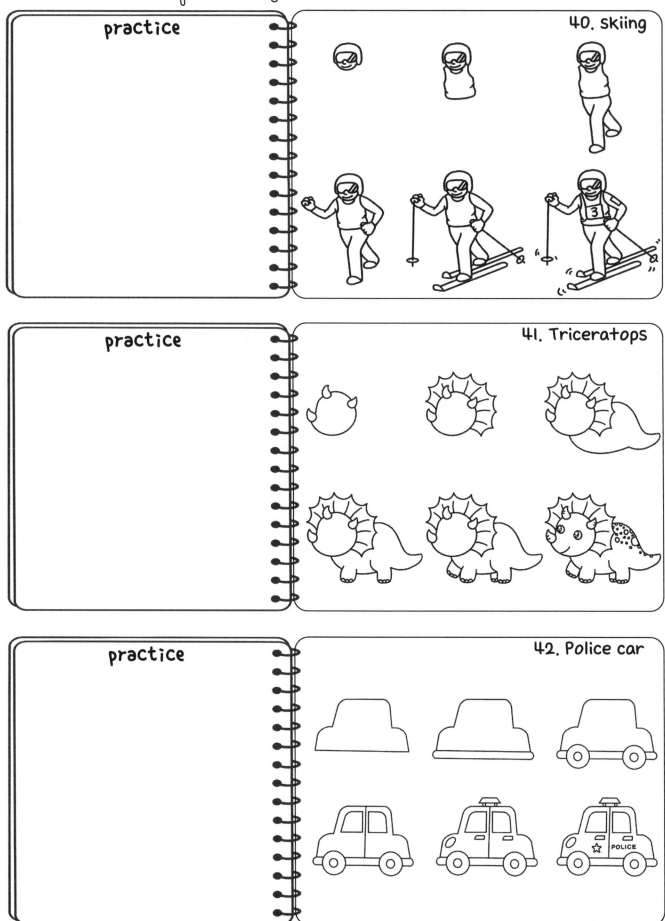

practice

40. skiing

practice

41. Triceratops

practice

42. Police car

POLICE

Let's draw a picture

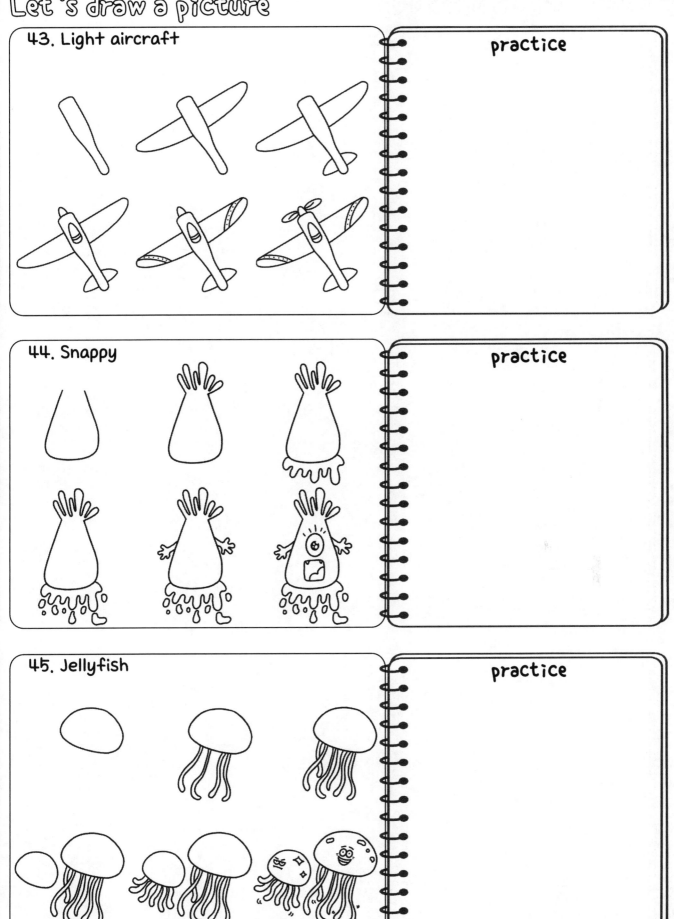

43. Light aircraft

practice

44. Snappy

practice

45. Jellyfish

practice

Let's draw a picture.

practice

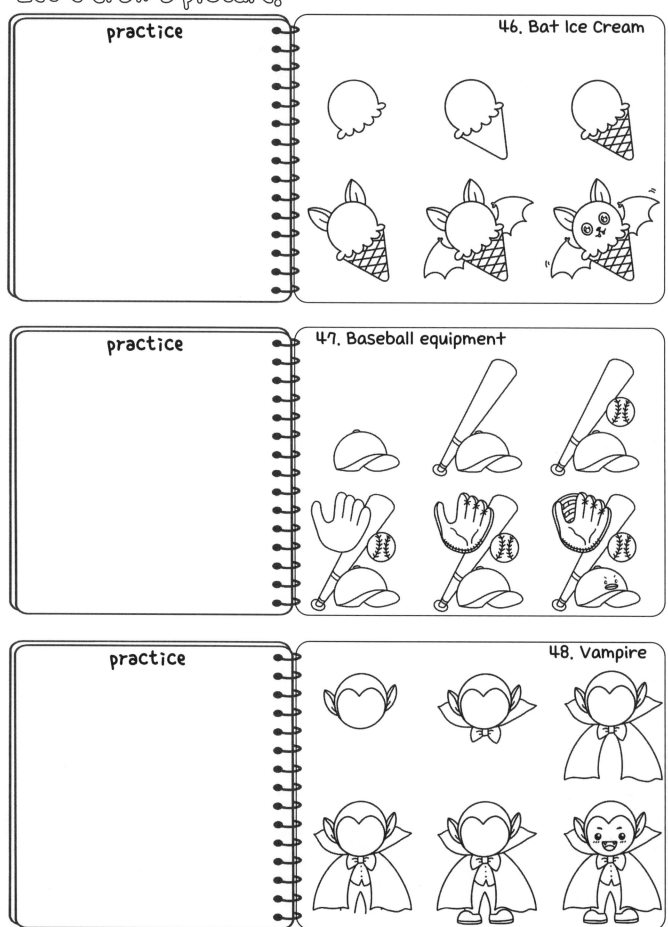

46. Bat Ice Cream

practice

47. Baseball equipment

practice

48. Vampire

Let's draw a picture

49. Surfing

50. Raccoon pirate

51. Treasure Box

Let's draw a picture .

practice

52. Pyramid

practice

53. Mummy

practice

54. bat Bunny

Let's draw a picture

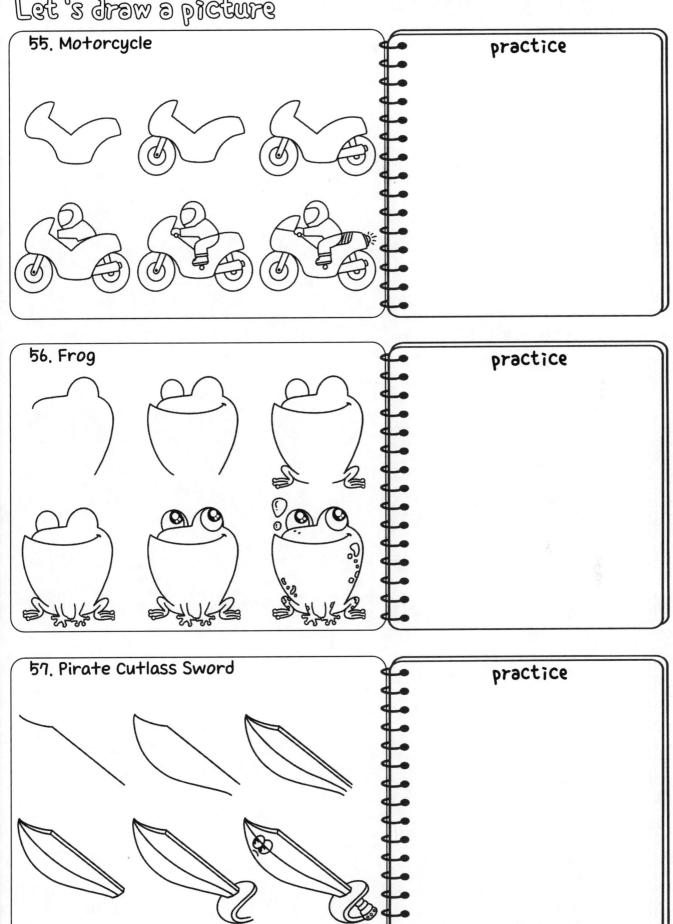

55. Motorcycle

practice

56. Frog

practice

57. Pirate Cutlass Sword

practice

Let's draw a picture.

practice

practice

practice

Let's draw a picture

61. Crab

practice

62. Tractor

practice

63. Capybara

practice

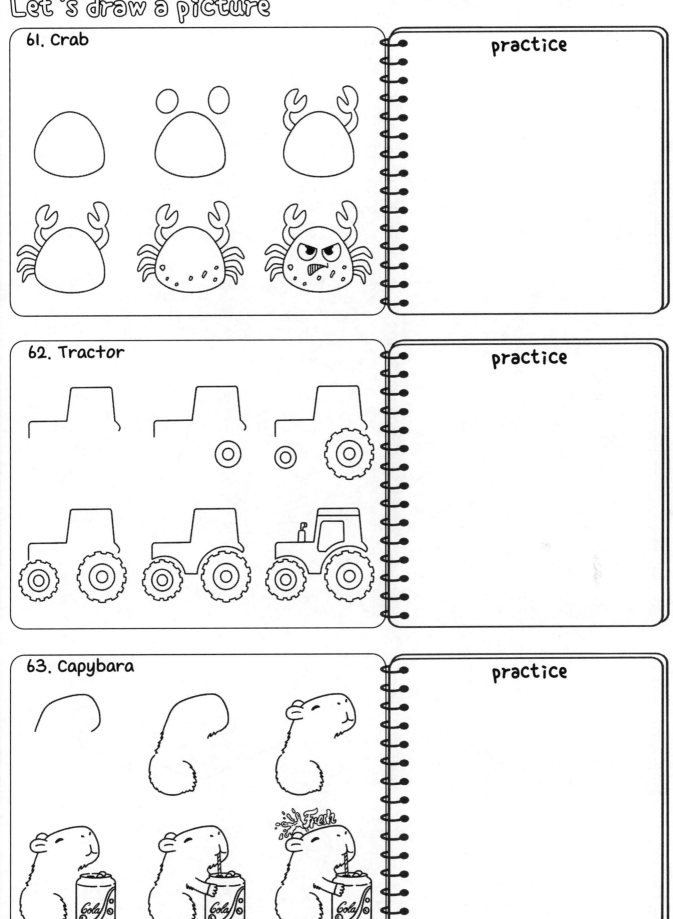

Let's draw a picture.

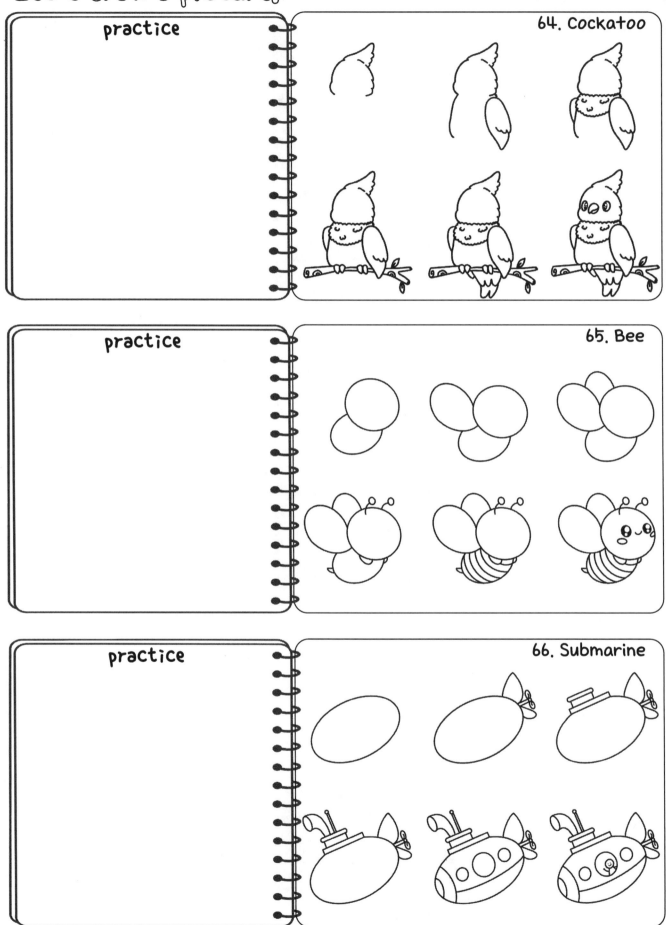

practice

64. Cockatoo

practice

65. Bee

practice

66. Submarine

Let's draw a picture

67. Baby Fox
practice

68. Whale Shark
practice

69. Voltix
practice

Let's draw a picture.

practice

practice

practice

70. Arctic Fox

71. Octopus

72. Gecko

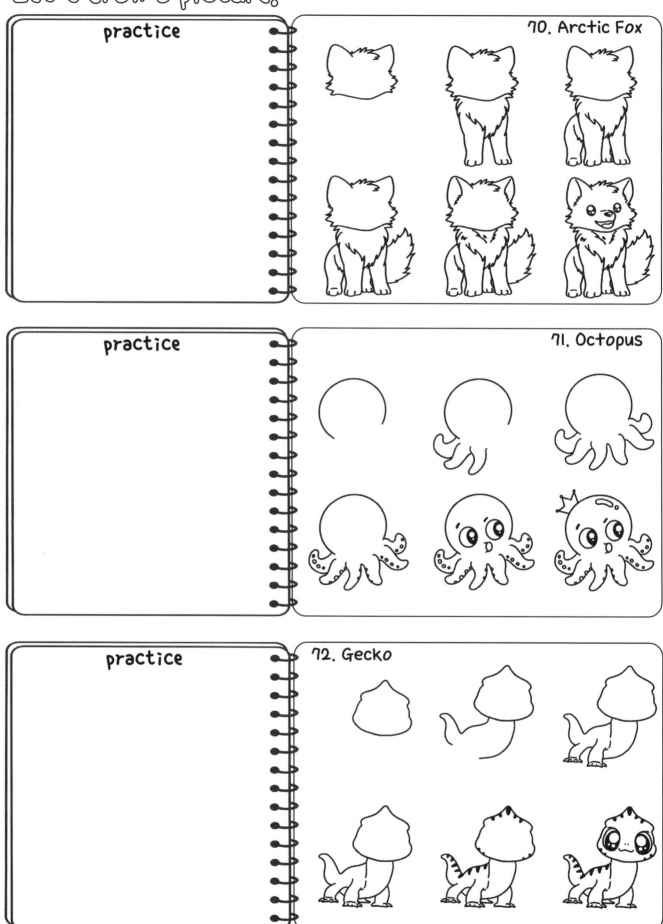

Let's draw a picture

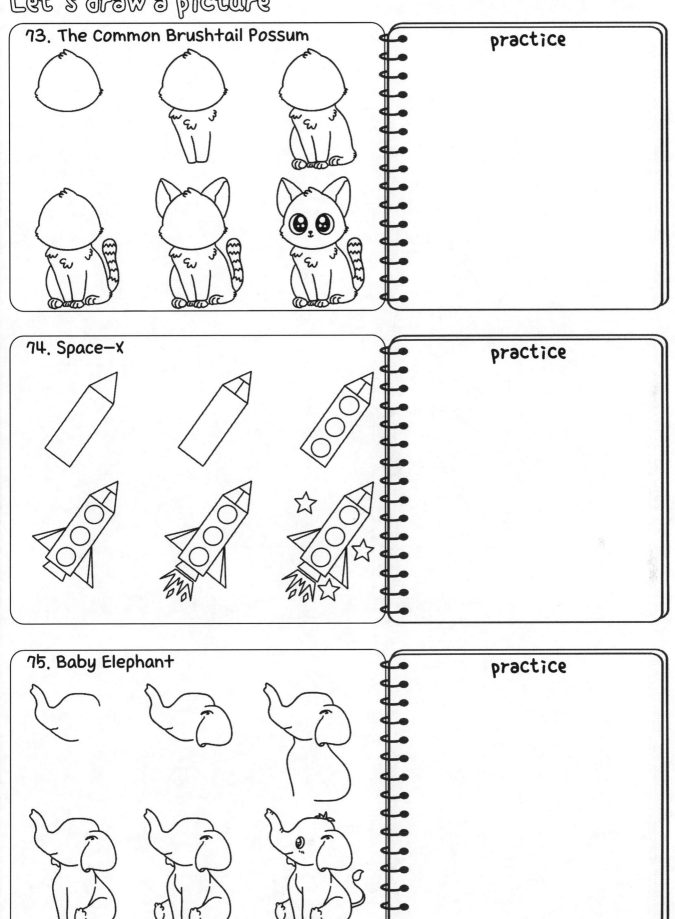

73. The Common Brushtail Possum

practice

74. Space-X

practice

75. Baby Elephant

practice

Let's draw a picture.

practice

76. Otter

practice

77. Hot air balloon

practice

78. Butterfly

Let's draw a picture

79. Pterosaur

80. Compact Car

81. Basketball

Let's draw a picture.

practice

82. Llama

practice

83. Anchor

practice

84. Frankenstein

Let's draw a picture

85. Miniature Schnauzer

practice

86. Firefighter

practice

87. Red Dragonfly

practice

Let's draw a picture.

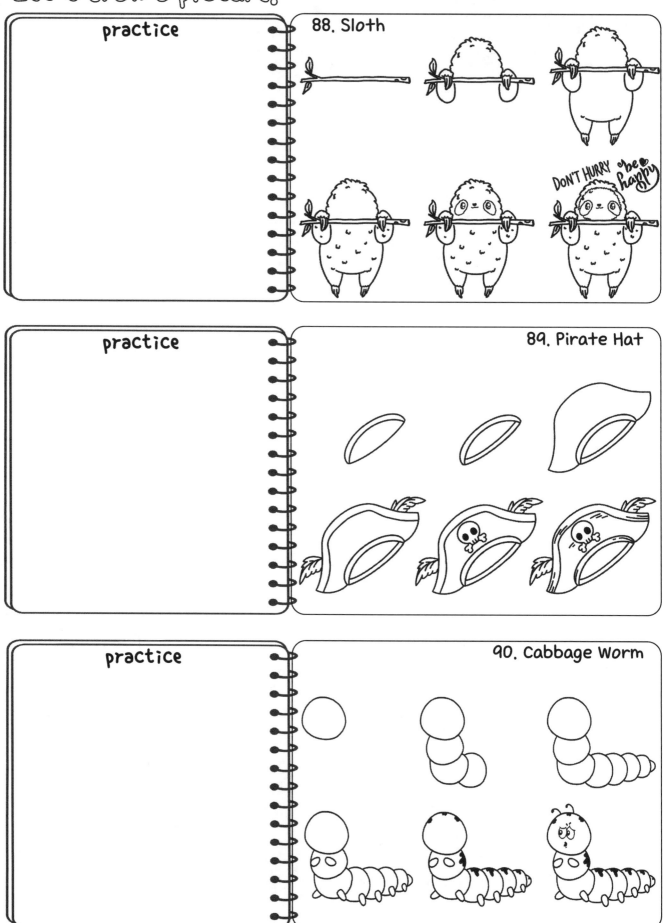

practice

88. Sloth

DON'T HURRY be happy

practice

89. Pirate Hat

practice

90. Cabbage Worm

Let's draw a picture

91. Desert Scorpion

practice

92. Tombstone

RIP

practice

93. Monarch Butterfly

practice

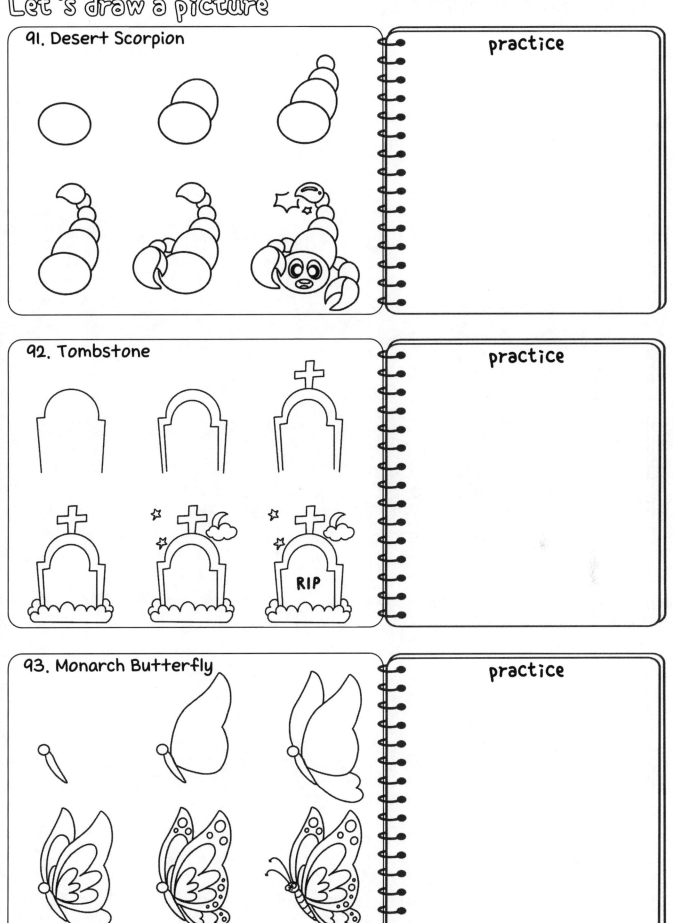

Let's draw a picture.

practice

94. Dachshund

Let's PLAY

practice

95. Fuzzy

practice

96. Cat

Let's draw a picture

97. Ziggy

98. Starfish

99. Wild Boar

Let's draw a picture.

practice

100. Sea Turtle

practice

101. Magic Ring

practice

102. Rocket

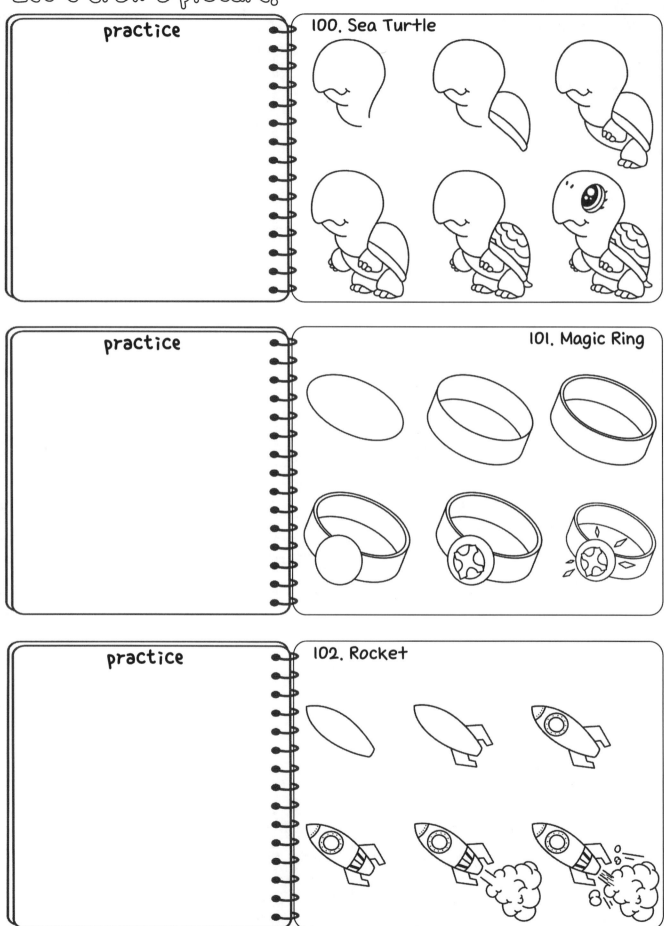

Let's draw a picture

103. Astronomical Telescope

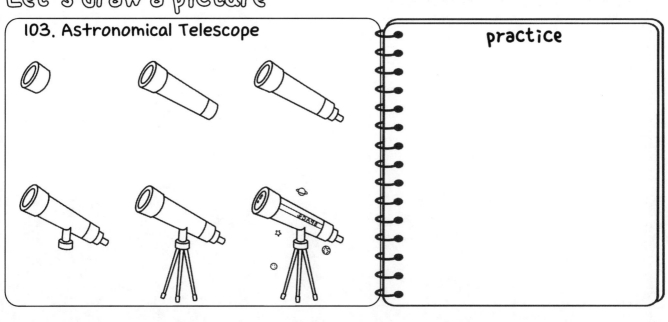

104. Parasaurolophus

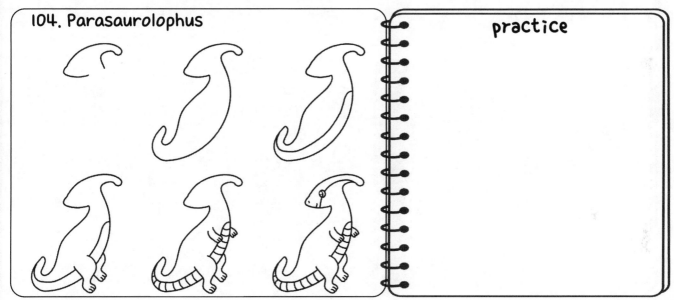

105. Fresh Juice

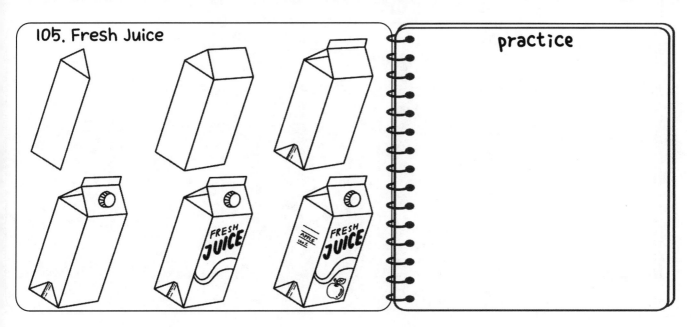

Let's draw a picture.

practice

107. Magical Sword

practice

108. centipede

practice

106. Cat

Let's draw a picture

109. Monkey

110. Godzilla

111. Wobbo

Let's draw a picture.

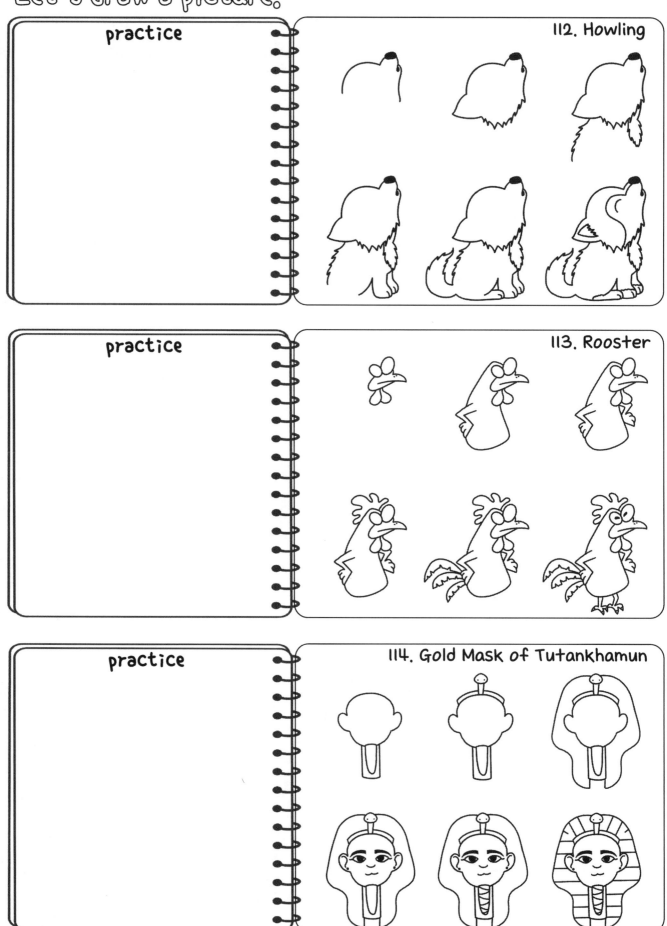

practice

112. Howling

practice

113. Rooster

practice

114. Gold Mask of Tutankhamun

Let's draw a picture

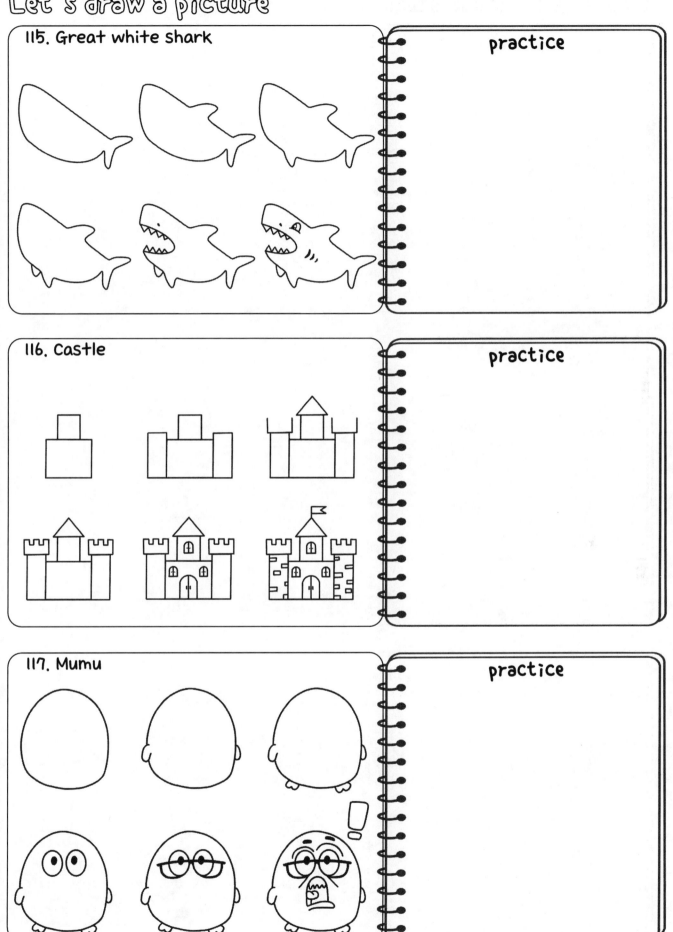

115. Great white shark

practice

116. Castle

practice

117. Mumu

practice

Let's draw a picture.

practice

118. Rhino

practice

119. Pippu(Acorn)

practice

120. Medieval Knight

Let's draw a picture

121. Giraffe

122. Frankenstein

123. Water

Let's draw a picture.

practice

124. Hippo

practice

125. Fitness Equipment

FITNESS

practice

126. Roman Soldier

Let's draw a picture

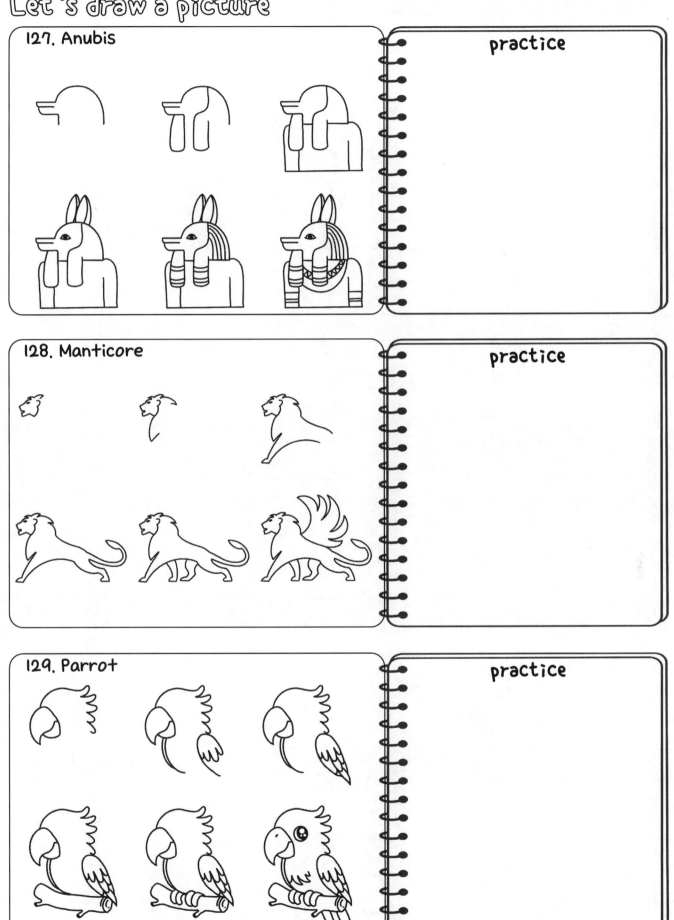

127. Anubis

practice

128. Manticore

practice

129. Parrot

practice

Let's draw a picture.

practice

130. Death

practice

131. Handheld Game Console

practice

132. Fire engine

Let's draw a picture

133. Hyena

practice

134. Fangor

practice

135. Ambulance

practice

Let's draw a picture.

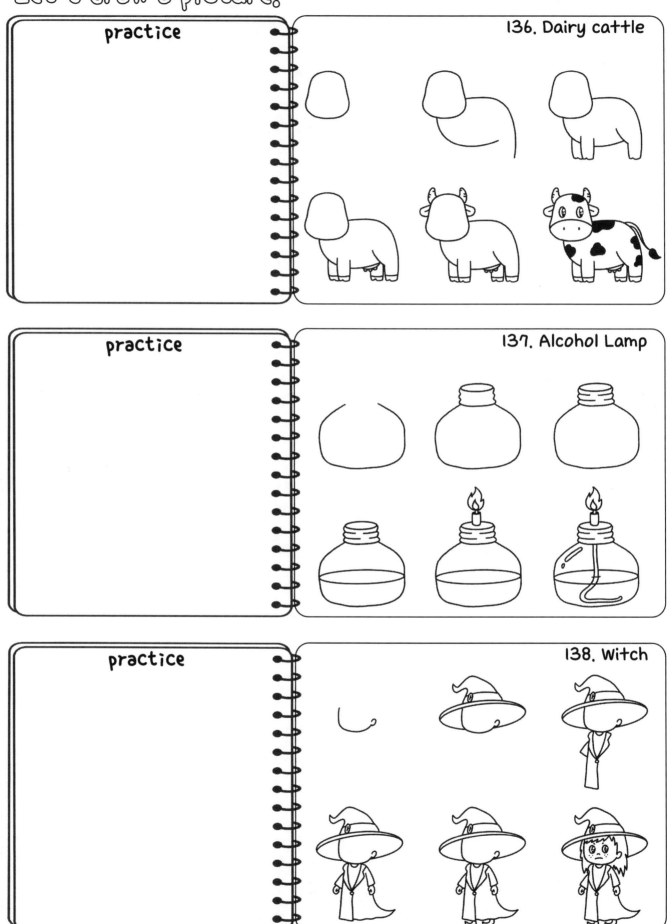

practice

136. Dairy cattle

practice

137. Alcohol Lamp

practice

138. Witch

Let's draw a picture

139. Triceratops

140. Cowboy Hat

141. Wolfric

Let's draw a picture.

practice

142. Lion

practice

143. Chemistry Experiments

practice

144. Dilophosaurus

Let's draw a picture

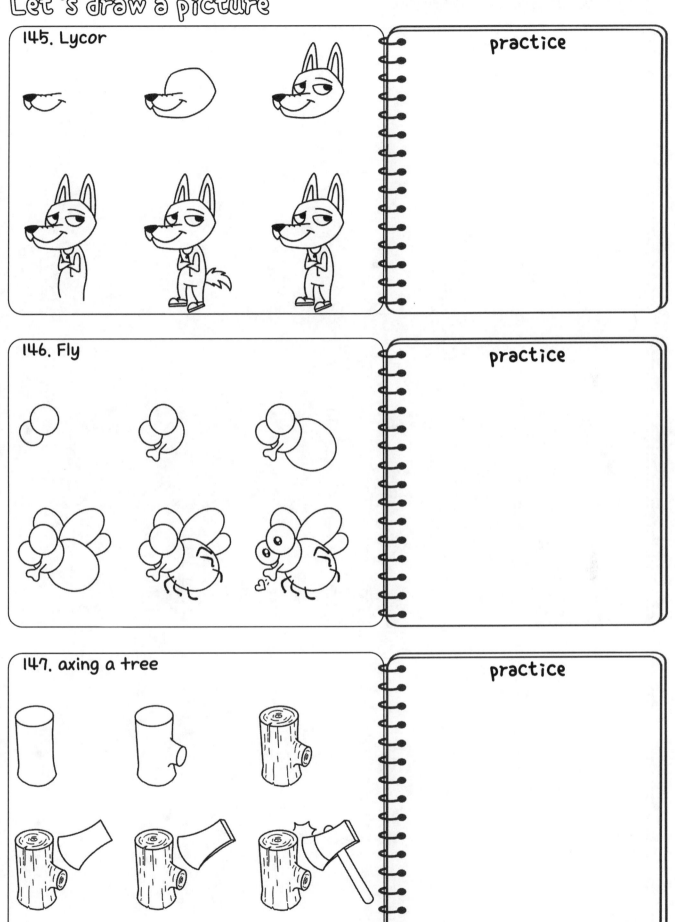

145. Lycor

practice

146. Fly

practice

147. axing a tree

practice

Let's draw a picture.

practice

148. Herbivorous Dinosaur

practice

149. Meerkat

practice

150. Skywing

Let's draw a picture

151. Kangaroo

practice

152. Tutu

practice

153. Angry Face

practice

Let's draw a picture.

practice

154. Satan

practice

155. Draknor

practice

156. Billy goat

Let's draw a picture

157. Gingerbread Men

158. Turkey

159. Skull Death

Let's draw a picture.

practice

160. Bull

practice

161. Petting a dog

practice

162. Armadillo

Let's draw a picture

163. True seal

practice

164. Chompillar

practice

165. Caterpillar

practice

Let's draw a picture.

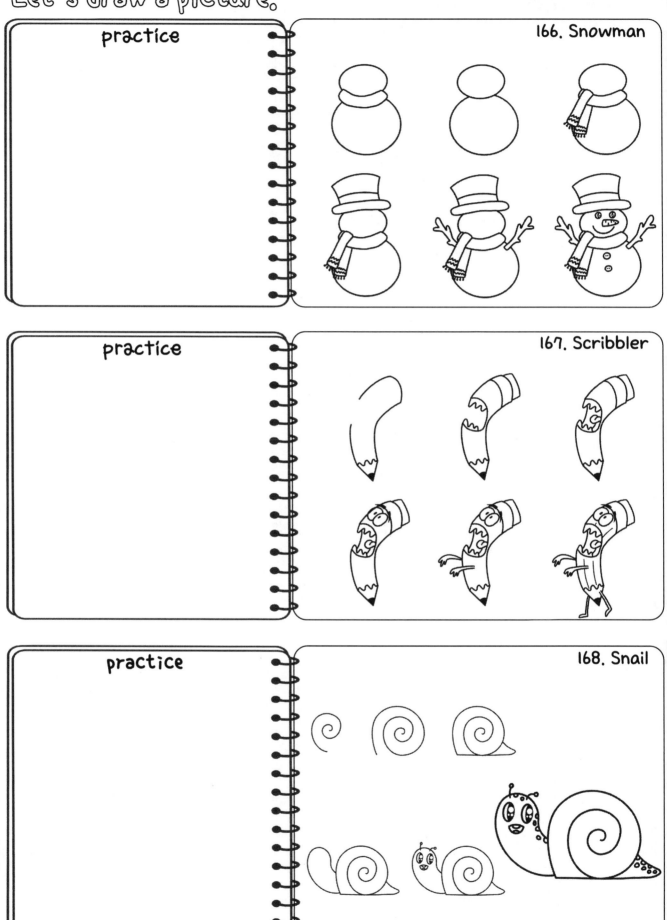

practice

166. Snowman

practice

167. Scribbler

practice

168. Snail

Let's draw a picture

169. Axolotl

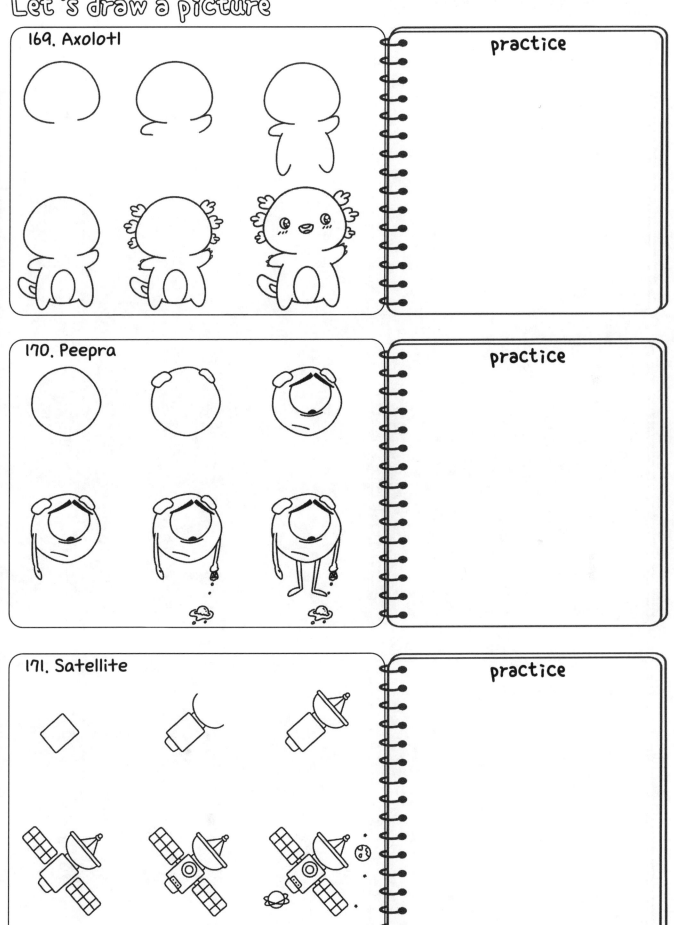

practice

170. Peepra

practice

171. Satellite

practice

Let's draw a picture.

practice

172. Pyrofang

practice

173. Surfing

practice

174. a chick watching a caterpillar

Let's draw a picture

175. Gloomshade

practice

176. Astronaut

practice

177. Camel

practice

Let's draw a picture.

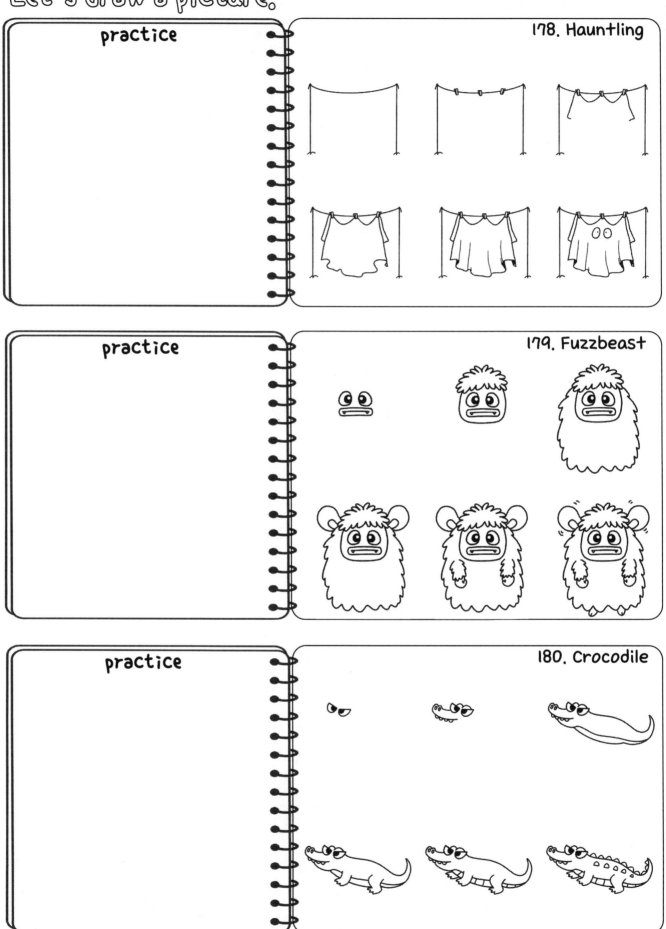

practice

178. Hauntling

practice

179. Fuzzbeast

practice

180. Crocodile

Let's draw a picture

181. Yark

182. Shagglor

183. Chameleon

Let's draw a picture.

practice

practice

practice

184. Ostrich

185. Glaregon

186. Tiger

Let's draw a picture

187. Quokka

practice

188. Swampfang

practice

189. Satellite Antenna

practice

Let's draw a picture.

practice

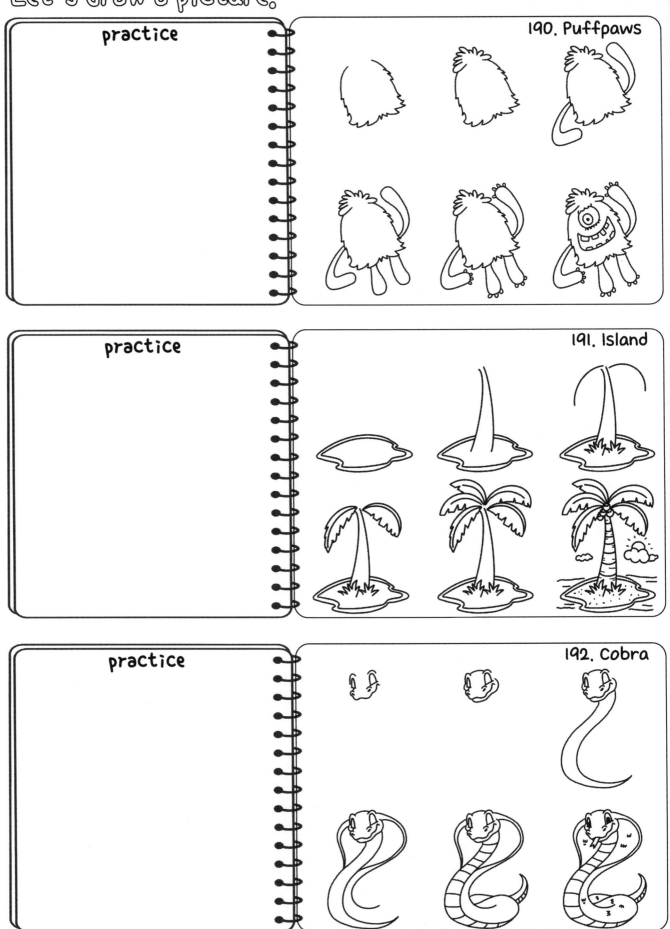

190. Puffpaws

practice

191. Island

practice

192. Cobra

Let's draw a picture

193. Duck

194. Shark

195. Tyrannosaur

Let's draw a picture.

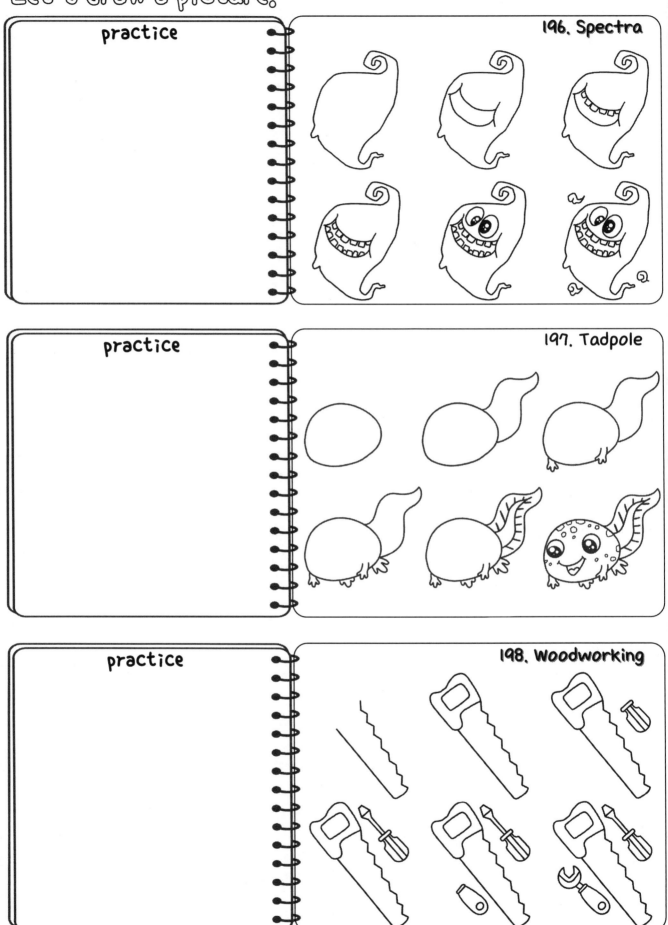

practice

196. Spectra

practice

197. Tadpole

practice

198. Woodworking

Let's draw a picture

199. kraken

200. Scorpion

201. Baby Dinosaur

Let's draw a picture.

practice

202. Giant panda

practice

203. Welsh Corgi

practice

204. Marshlurker

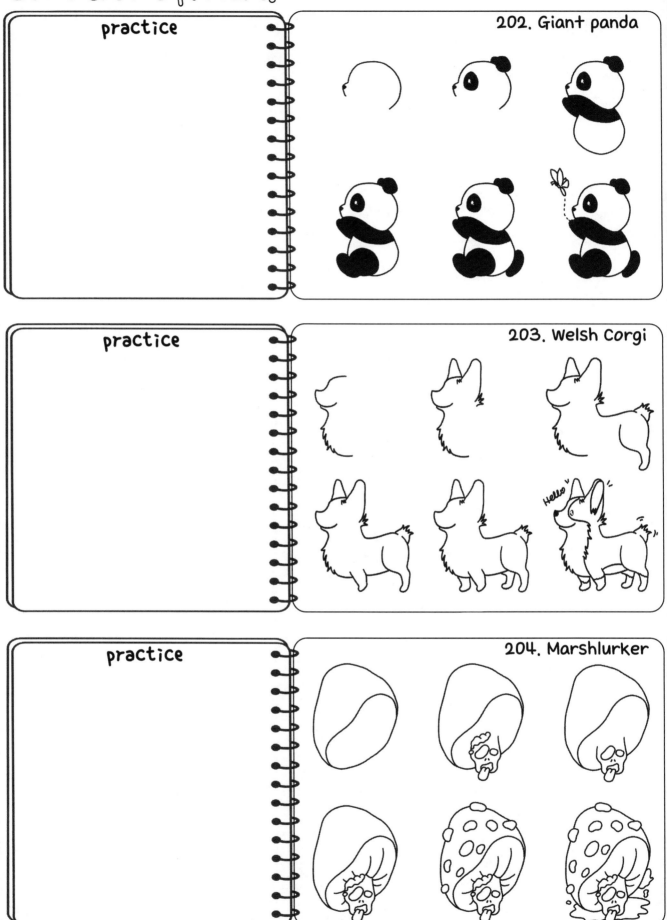

Let's draw a picture

205. Viking

practice

206. Hedgehog

practice

207. Spider

practice

Let's draw a picture.

practice

208. Vampire Bee

practice

209. Dwarf

practice

210. Eagle

Let's draw a picture

211. Hadrosaurus

212. Puffdragon

213. Mimic

practice

practice

practice

Let's draw a picture.

practice

214. Boxing Gloves

practice

215. Zebra

practice

216. Samurai Skull

Let's draw a picture

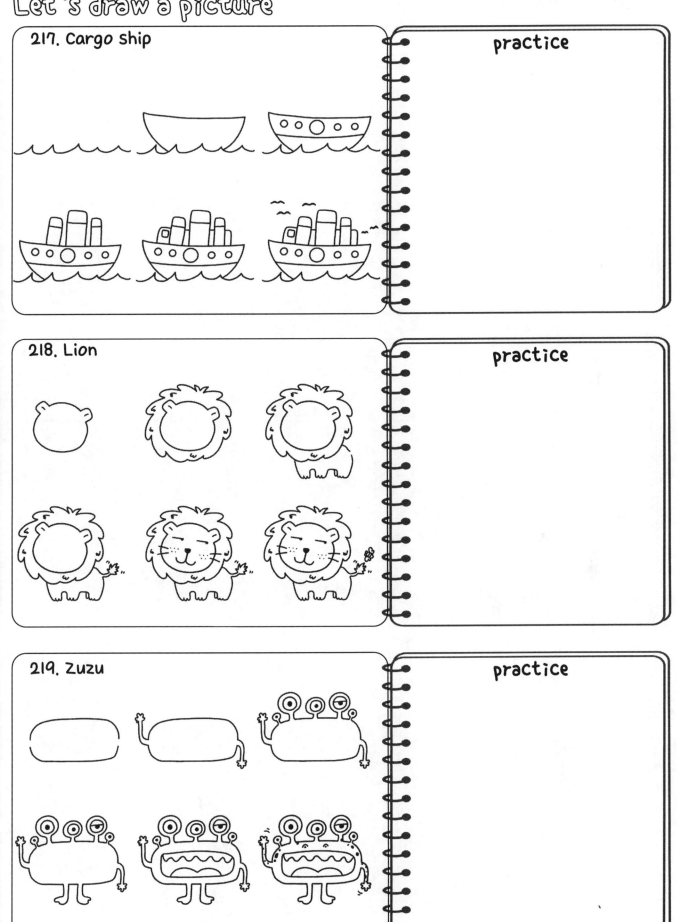

217. Cargo ship

practice

218. Lion

practice

219. Zuzu

practice

Let's draw a picture.

practice

220. Witch Cat

practice

221. Fawn

practice

222. Pirate Parrot

Let's draw a picture

223. Hammer & Wrench

practice

224. spotted ray

practice

225. Fluffkin

practice

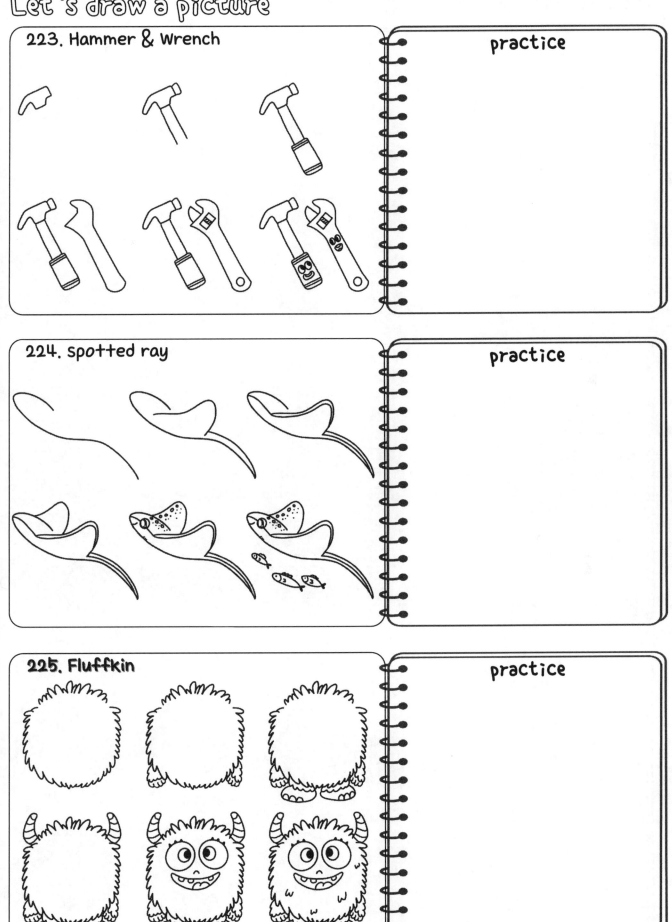

Let's draw a picture.

practice

226. Kickboard

practice

227. Viking Warrior

practice

228. Mammoth

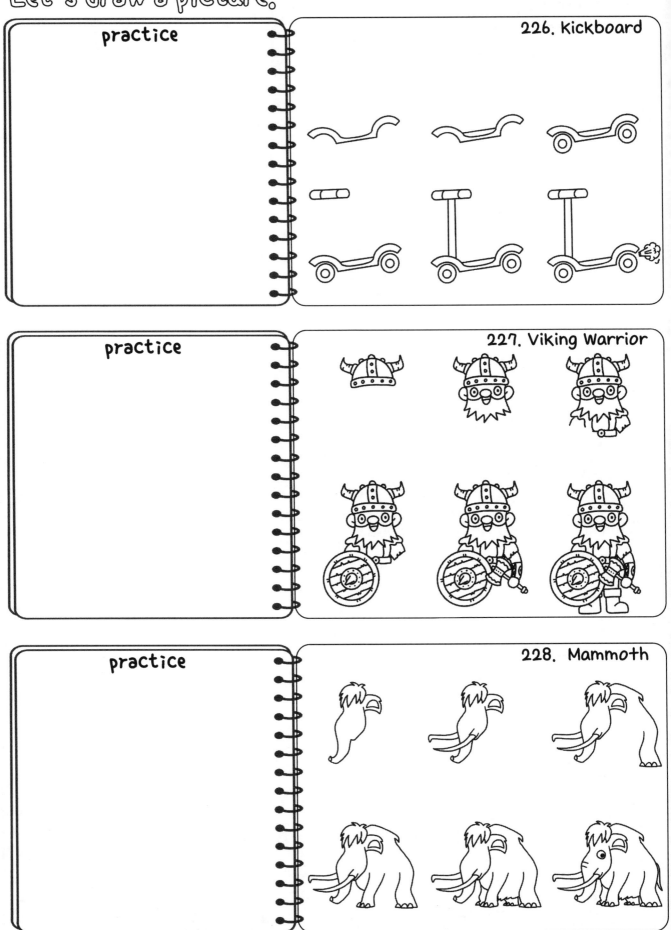

Let's draw a picture

229. Plesiosaurus

230. Cat riding a skateboard

231. Phantasm

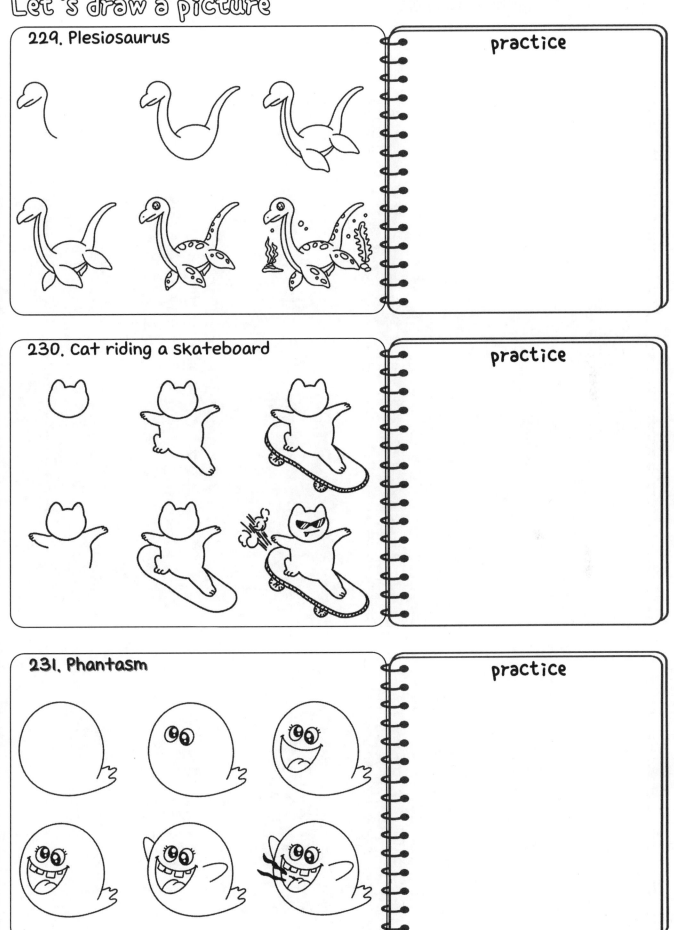

Let's draw a picture.

practice

232. Compass

practice

233. Stegosaurus

practice

234. Ghost Pumpkin

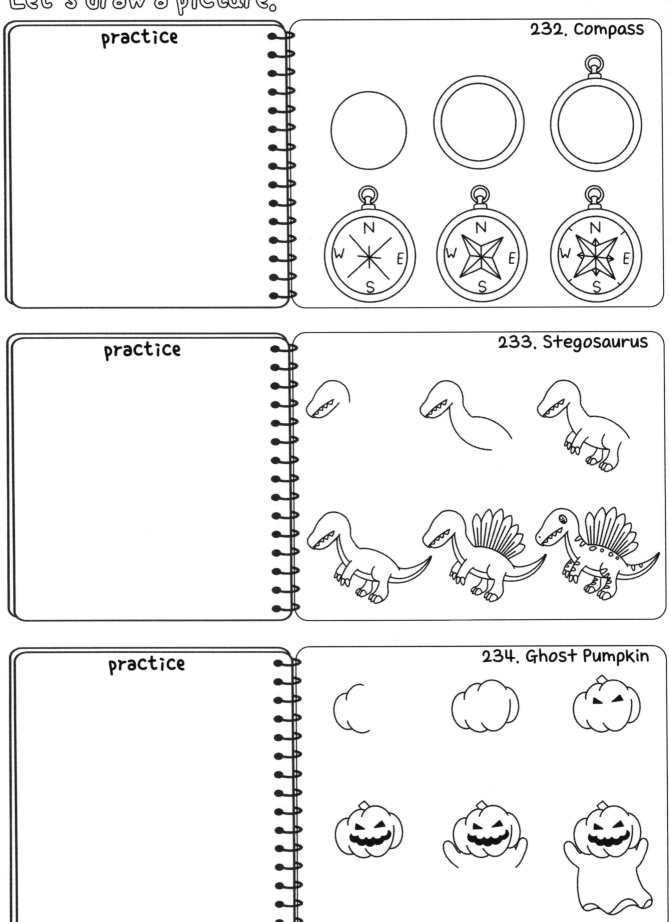

Let's draw a picture

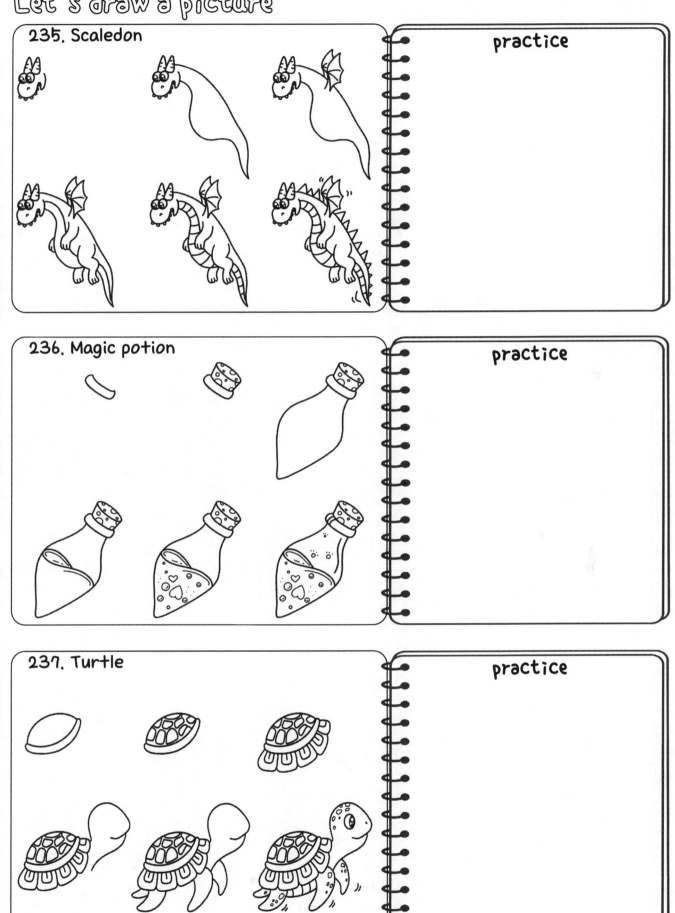

235. Scaledon

practice

236. Magic potion

practice

237. Turtle

practice

Let's draw a picture.

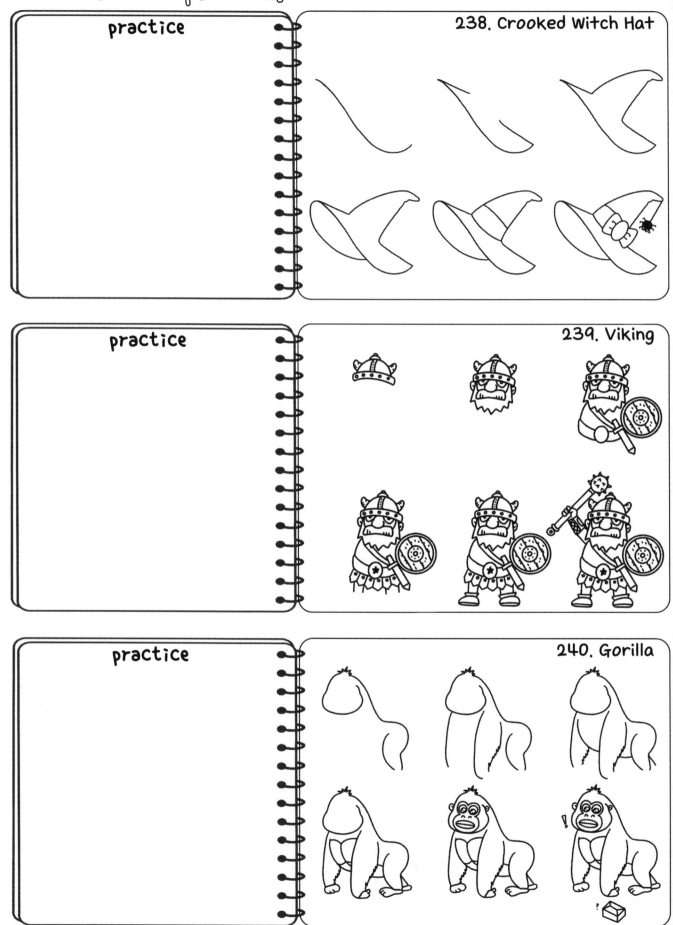

practice

238. Crooked Witch Hat

practice

239. Viking

practice

240. Gorilla

Draw your imagination!

Draw your imagination!